ML ++
593.6 R137 2006
Rake, Jody Sullivan.
Sea anemones

WITHDRAWN

P9-CSE-922

Pebble™ Plus

Under the Sea

Sea Anemones

Rake, Jody Sullivan

by Jody Sullivan

Consulting Editor: Gail Saunders-Smith, PhD

Consultant: Debbie Nuzzolo, Education Manager
SeaWorld, San Diego, California

Capstone press

Mankato, Minnesota

Pebble Plus is published by Capstone Press,
151 Good Counsel Drive, P.O. Box 669, Mankato, Minnesota 56002.
www.capstonepress.com

Copyright © 2006 by Capstone Press. All rights reserved.
No part of this publication may be reproduced in whole or in part, or stored in a retrieval system, or
transmitted in any form or by any means, electronic, mechanical, photocopying, recording, or otherwise,
without written permission of the publisher. For information regarding permission, write to Capstone Press,
151 Good Counsel Drive, P.O. Box 669, Dept. R, Mankato, Minnesota 56002.
Printed in the United States of America

1 2 3 4 5 6 10 09 08 07 06 05

Library of Congress Cataloging-in-Publication Data
Sullivan, Jody.
    Sea anemones / by Jody Sullivan.
    p. cm.—(Pebble plus. Under the sea)
    Summary: "Simple text and photographs present sea anemones, where they live, how they
look, and what they do"—Provided by publisher.
    Includes bibliographical references and index.
    ISBN 0-7368-4271-3 (hardcover)
    1. Sea anemones—Juvenile literature. I. Title. II. Series: Under the sea (Mankato, Minn.)
QL377.C7S87 2006
593.6—dc22   2004026904

Editorial Credits

Martha E. H. Rustad and Aaron Sautter, editors; Juliette Peters, set designer; Kate Opseth, book designer;
    Kelly Garvin, photo researcher; Scott Thoms, photo editor

Photo Credits

Bruce Coleman Inc./Bill Wood, 8–9
Corbis/Brandon D. Cole, cover
Corel, 1
James P. Rowan, 11
Jeff Rotman, 12–13
Marty Snyderman, 15, 19
Pete Carmichael, 16–17
Seapics.com/David Wrobel, 7; Dean & Sharon Williams, 20–21
Tom Stack & Associates, Inc./Brian Parker, 4–5

Note to Parents and Teachers

The Under the Sea set supports national science standards related to the diversity and
unity of life. This book describes and illustrates sea anemones. The images support
early readers in understanding the text. The repetition of words and phrases helps early
readers learn new words. This book also introduces early readers to subject-specific
vocabulary words, which are defined in the Glossary section. Early readers may need
assistance to read some words and to use the Table of Contents, Glossary, Read More,
Internet Sites, and Index sections of the book.

FOND DU LAC PUBLIC LIBRARY

Table of Contents

What Are Sea Anemones?

Sea anemones

are sea animals.

They have many tentacles.

tentacle

Sea anemones stick to rocks
and coral reefs.

Some sea anemones are
as big as a car tire.
Other sea anemones are
as small as your fingernail.

Body Parts

Sea anemones have

soft bodies.

They do not have bones.

11

Sea anemones have a mouth

in the center of their bodies.

mouth

Sea anemones have
many tentacles that sting.

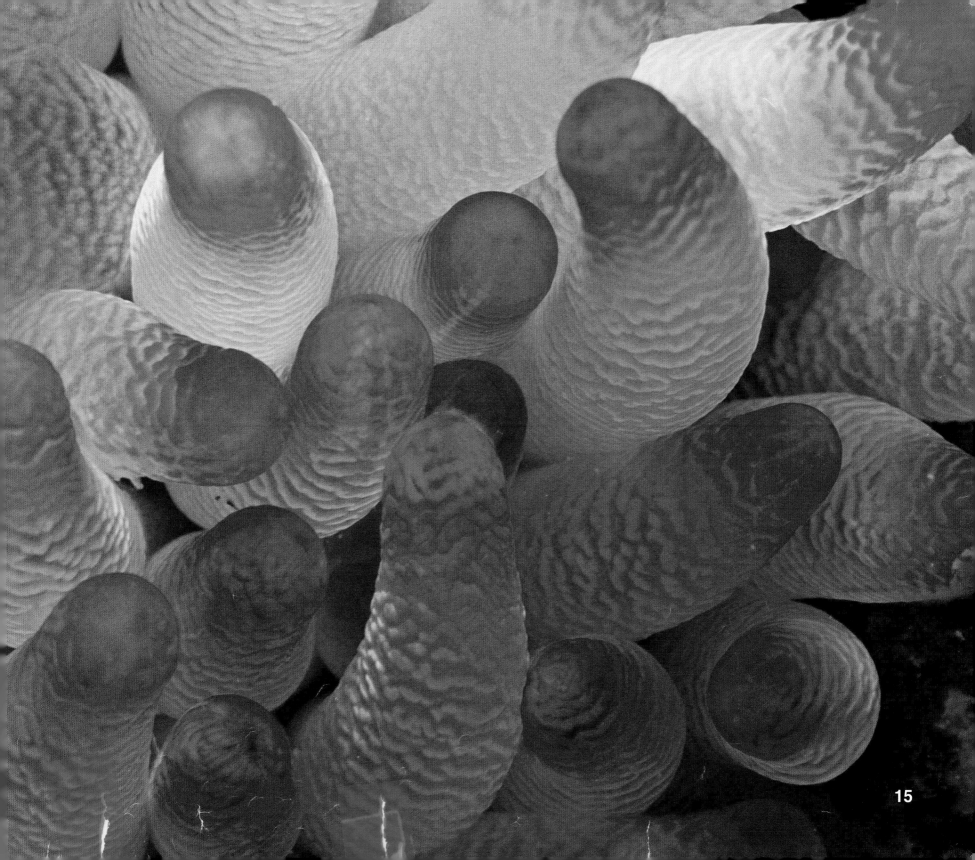

What Sea Anemones Do

Sea anemones sting prey
with their tentacles.
The tentacles pull prey
into the anemone's mouth.

17

Some sea anemones are
homes for clown fish.
Clown fish have
a layer of slime.
It keeps them
safe from the stings.

Under the Sea

Sea anemones live
in tide pools and
under the sea.

Glossary

clown fish—a small tropical fish that lives in the tentacles of sea anemones

coral reef—an area of coral skeletons and rocks in shallow ocean water

prey—an animal hunted by another animal for food; sea anemones eat fish and other animals.

sting—to hurt with a poisoned tip; sea anemones sting prey with their tentacles.

tentacle—a long, flexible arm of an animal

tide pool—a small pool that forms at low tide on rocky beaches

Read More

Lindeen, Carol K. *Clown Fish.* Pebble Plus: Under the Sea. Mankato, Minn.: Capstone Press, 2005.

Schaefer, Lola M. *Sea Anemones.* Ooey-Gooey Animals. Chicago: Heinemann Library, 2002.

Stone, Lynn M. *Sea Anemones.* Vero Beach, Fla.: Rourke, 2003.

Internet Sites

FactHound offers a safe, fun way to find Internet sites related to this book. All of the sites on FactHound have been researched by our staff.

Here's how:

1. Visit *www.facthound.com*

2. Type in this special code **0736842713** for age-appropriate sites. Or enter a search word related to this book for a more general search.

3. Click on the **Fetch It** button.

FactHound will fetch the best sites for you!

Index

Word Count: 111
Grade: 1
Early-Intervention Level: 14